101

Crafty Activities

for 3-5-year-olds

Published by Crossbridge Books
Worcester
www.crossbridgeeducational.com

ISBN 978-1-913946-85-2

British Library Cataloguing Publication Data

A catalogue record for this book is available from the British Library

CROSSBRIDGE
BOOKS

101
Crafty Activities
for 3-5-year-olds

R M Price-Mohr

Contents: Page

Introduction

The ideas suggested in this book are all possible with very little cost; any extra household items that you might need should be easily available in supermarkets. All the ideas have been tried and tested with my own children, my grandchildren, or in my former childcare settings.

Some of these activities are 'messy play', so you will need to be prepared to make a space ready, maybe on a tiled floor where you can clean up afterwards, and put your little one in clothes that don't matter or put on an apron if you have one.

Much of the materials used are designed to be 'recycle play'. Most people will have used yoghurt pots or dip pots, old delivery or food boxes, egg boxes, kitchen towel, cardboard tubes, drinks cartons, newspapers, and magazines.

Children understand role play and can join in with storytelling from a very young age. Some of the activities are designed to be for 'imaginative play'. So long as you animate an object (make it seem alive by moving it), you can role play with almost anything – you could even take your sock off, put it over your hand and create an instant glove puppet – so long as it moves it will appear to become alive and will stimulate your child's imagination.

The activities are themed but are in no particular order (except the Great Big Enormous Turnip).

Messy play

Water

Water play is the easiest messy play to set up, so long as you have a plastic bowl. If you have bubble bath this makes it more fun. Make sure you are prepared for the splashing so that you can both play with freedom.

If you have some plastic toys, maybe bath toys, make use of them. If you have things that are safe to play with but sink it doesn't matter, in fact this will give your child an early grasp of sinking and floating.

Floating/sinking

Set up a bowl full of clear water and collect child-safe objects to test to see if they float or sink. Help your child to sort the objects into two piles.

Margarine tub Moses' basket

Using a cleaned-out margarine tub (or similar), glue long leaves (or strips of paper) around the outside. Using more leaves (or paper), create a soft mattress inside. Next you can make a baby out of plasticine or play dough.

Make blankets by rolling out the plasticine or play dough very thinly so that it can be wrapped around. You can now float it on the water.

Floating/sinking

Fill a clear jar with water. Gently put in a fresh egg and wait for it to sink. Now gradually add cheap cooking salt, stirring it in until it dissolves. Watch the egg rise.

Floating fish

Using the same salt water, you can now make a fishbowl. Cut out fish shapes using cardboard from frozen food cartons (these are waxy and waterproof). On the blank side colour using wax crayons.

Using different sized paper clips, experiment to see which level your fish will float at (bigger paper clips will make your fish sink lower).

Floating/sinking

Fill a tumbler with fizzy water or lemonade. Let your child add raisins or sultanas one at a time. As the bubbles attach themselves to the dried fruit, you will see them rise to the top. When they reach the top, the gas in the bubbles disperses and the fruit will sink again before collecting more bubbles and going back up again.

If you have food colouring, add a drop to make it more exciting. If you have several colours, you could put them in a row in front of the window and they will keep going for hours.

Paper boat

Using a square of paper, ask your child to decorate it with geometric patterns using thick wax crayon on both sides. Now you can make your boat and test to see if it floats.

Food colouring is something you can use for a lot of these activities. If your child is old enough to blow through a straw, put some colouring in some water in a bowl – with a drop of bubble bath – and blow some bubbles.

If you have any spare paper in the house, you could even make a bubble print. An old white envelope would do – just lay it over the bubbles and allow them a moment to stain the paper.

Alternatively, mix washing-up liquid with watered-down paint. Using a straw, blow the paint into bubbles. Carefully place a sheet of paper over to make a bubble print.

Paint blowing

Put blobs of runny watered-down paint on some paper. Using a straw, blow the paint into patterns or shapes. If you use different colours, they will run into each other and mix for a good effect.

Gloop

This messy gloop is made from cornflour. Mix it with a small amount of water and have fun exploring how it feels. When you squeeze it, it seems quite solid, but when you open your hand, it will drip away.

Try adding some food colouring to make it more exciting. You can even mix in some breakfast cereal to get a different feel.

If your child has any small toys that can survive being wet, they can join in the fun too. Very young children will just enjoy the experience of the texture, but older ones can create landscapes and let their imagination run wild.

Jelly is a great alternative to cornflour gloop. Try adding some frozen peas to the mixture, it creates another texture.

Again, you can put some toys into the landscape; plastic dinosaurs are a great idea for this one if you have them.

Play dough can easily be made at home and stored in the fridge.

You will need:

- 8 tablespoons of flour
- 2 tablespoons of salt
- 60ml warm water
- 1 tablespoon of vegetable oil
- Food colouring

Mix the flour and salt in a bowl. In a separate bowl, mix together the water, oil and food colouring.

Pour the coloured water into the flour mix and bind together with a spoon.

Knead the mixture on a floured surface until it is smooth, soft dough.

You can use raisins or currants to make faces.

Paint and glue

Finger painting is always a great activity, especially if you don't have any paint brushes at home. But what if you don't have any paint either?

Here are some ideas for making your own paint – and all of them are safe and edible. The paint in the picture above was made with yoghurt.

- Plain yoghurt mixed with food colouring
- Flour, water, and food colouring
- 2 parts cornflour, 3 parts white vinegar and food colouring

Experiment and see which you prefer.

Gluing and sticking is always fun, but what if you don't have any glue? Here is a recipe for home-made glue:

You will need

- 3 tablespoons of flour
- 1 tablespoon of sugar
- 1 tablespoon of salt
- 3 tablespoons of water
- a Bain Marie (a bowl of hot water that is larger than your mixing bowl)

Slowly mix the flour into the cold water. Stand your mixing bowl inside the Bain Marie and gradually add the sugar and salt, stirring all the time until the salt and sugar are dissolved.

You can cut out or tear shapes from a newspaper or magazine and together you can stick them on to left-over cardboard or contrasting pages in a magazine.

Nature play

Plants and leaves

Your garden or the local park can be a great source of materials for activities that also get you out of the house when you go on your nature resource hunts.

Make a garden-on-a-plate

Using a water-proof plate, collect some moss and pebbles to make the grass and edging for your miniature garden.

Dig up some wild flowers (not protected ones) such as daisies, making sure that you include the roots, and put them in amongst the moss. Using a small flower pot (or yoghurt pot), plant some flower seeds and put the pot in your garden.

Water the pot and the moss (without flooding the plate). Remember to keep watering and watch your garden grow.

Miniature garden in a jar

You will need an old jar or cut down plastic bottle. Put a layer of small stones on the bottom. Next put in a layer of soil.

Now you need to look for small plants; wild plants are fine. If you can find moss, put some on the top to keep in the moisture. Don't forget to water it.

Bugs for the miniature garden

You will need some old card, (greetings cards are best) and some flimsy black paper (from magazines is best). Help your child to cut out egg shapes from the card for the bug bodies. Next you will probably need to help with cutting out the black paper legs as shown in the picture. Help your child to cut out some small circles for eyes. Next you need a short narrow strip of paper folded concertina style with just three folds. Glue one end onto the black legs and the other end onto the underneath of the body so that the legs stand out from the body. Glue on the eyes.

To make wings, use celephane from sweet wrappers or food containers. Make two short slits and push it through. If you have cocktail or lolly sticks, stick them to the underneath of the card body (keeping the black legs separate). When you jiggle your bugs, the legs should move.

Leaf picture

On a plate or tray, mix up some plain flour and water to make a sticky base so that you can stick your leaves on to make a pattern or picture.

If you have a printer, you could take a photo and print the picture to display on the wall.

Out and about

Collect some straight sticks and leaves of different shapes and sizes.

Tie two sticks together to make a cross (I used an elastic band to do this). Next draw and cut out a head and wide neck shape out of old card. Cut a little way into the neck piece so that you can wrap and tape it around the top part of the upright stick. Now you can use the leaves to make a puppet.

As an alternative you could draw/colour a face or stick one on from a magazine or old greeting card.

Catkins, a coat of many colours, and a plastic bottle

If you still have your two sticks and the cardboard cut-out, you can use these, or you can use a wooden spoon. The catkins in the picture were collected from the garden; if you can't get these, you could use wool or string to make some hair.

Using an old plastic bottle, stand your stick person inside so that it can stand by itself. Now you can dress it. To make a coat like the one shown above, draw a rainbow on a large sheet of paper. Next fold it in half and paint one side of it. While the paint is still wet, fold it in half and carefully press together so that you get a symmetrical print on the other half. Cut out the semicircle you have painted and wrap it around the plastic bottle. You could make a whole family of stick people to play with.

Stick-and-leaf scarecrow

Find two straight sticks that you can make into a cross. Next, using some old card cut out a head and a short coat with sleeves and attach to the cross. (I used an elastic band round the neck and slid it over the top for the head. The coat was paper-clipped into place.)

Next find some leaves – large ones for the coat and spiky ones for the hair – and glue them on.

Finally give your scarecrow a face.

Morris the scarecrow

Using two straight sticks make a cross. Using an old large envelope, make a hole for the neck and arms and slot it over the sticks. This can be decorated with colourful strips of paper to look like a Morris dancer's 'raggy jacket'.

Next, inflate a balloon for the head. Use a cardboard tube for the neck and attach the balloon through the tube with an elastic band to keep the head upright. Paint on the face. Next make a hat. I have used two paper plates. This can be painted and decorated like a Morris hat. Add some fringes of hair.

Finally, put him in the garden

Pots

Spotty pots

Using yoghurt pots or cut-down water bottles, make containers for plants from the garden. You could add flowers you have made. Using sand paper or a metal scourer, rub over the surface to make it rough, this will help the paint to stick. Help your child to give the pot a first coat and wait for it to dry.

While it is drying you could be collecting your plants from the garden. When your pots are dry, give them a second coat. While you are waiting for them to dry again, practise making your spot prints. Cut the end off a carrot, dip it in paint and print your spots. Practise on an old piece of card. When your second coat is dry, help your child to print the spots in a contrasting colour.

Flower-pot men

You can use either real clay flower pots or yoghurt pots covered and/or painted. Use a potato for the body. Make holes for the arms – you can use straws or pipe cleaners.

Next, using a cocktail stick connect the potato with a small onion for the head.

Next make a hat. I have used an egg box carton – this can be painted or decorated (I have attached a flower. I have also used hyacinth flowers for the hands.) Finally give your flower-pot man a face.

Stones

L ittle Tommy Tittlemouse
Lived in a little house;
He caught fishes
In other men's ditches.

Ladybug stones

Find some smooth stones of different sizes. It doesn't matter if they are not a perfect shape. Help your child to wash them and have a good look at the natural colours and texture.

When they are dry, you can paint them to make a family of lady birds or any other creature that you prefer. They can now be placed in your garden or in a tub.

Washed stones snail

Make a collection of stones of different sizes. Help your child to wash them thoroughly – this is the fun bit! Next help your child to put them in order of size starting with the smallest.

Next, using some old card, cut out a large snail shape. Using long strings of plasticine (or something similar) lay out a spiral where the shell will go.

Now the stones can be pushed onto the plasticine in a spiral, starting in the middle with the smallest stone.

Snake in the grass

Using magazines, help your child to cut out long 'grass' blades from pictures that are mostly green. Next they can be glued to cardboard tubes that have been cut to different heights. These can be placed together as clumps of grass.

Next, using the washed stones, help your child to sort them. For example, I had three groups: white, brown and grey stones. Ask your child to place them in sequence in a wiggly line to be a snake in the grass.

You could glue on some eyes and a tongue.

Frogs on stepping stones

Using magazines, help your child to cut out large pieces of blue, cut with wavy lines. These can be overlapped to create a pond.

Next, using the washed stones, help your child to find six flatish stones that can be stepping stones across the pond. The rest of the stones can be arranged around the edge of the pond. (If you made the snake grass, you could add these as water reeds).

Next, using plasticine, or similar, make six little frogs to sit on the stepping stones. To make the frogs make one large ball for the body, then two small sausage shapes for the legs.

Next make two small balls for the eyes. Using your thumbnail, press a line into each eye ball as shown.

Building a stone wall

Using your collection of stones, help your child to build a wall. I have used plastercine as mortar to hold the stones together, but you could use play dough, flour dough, or even get some mud and sand and mix some real mortar.

Next, make the sheep. Using the inside of old greetings cards or other thin card, copy the image shown. Cut out around the top of head and the ears and around the chin, but be careful not to cut across the bold section on the head (otherwise it will fall off!). Your child can stick on some cotton wool and colour the ears and/or face grey or black.

Twigs

 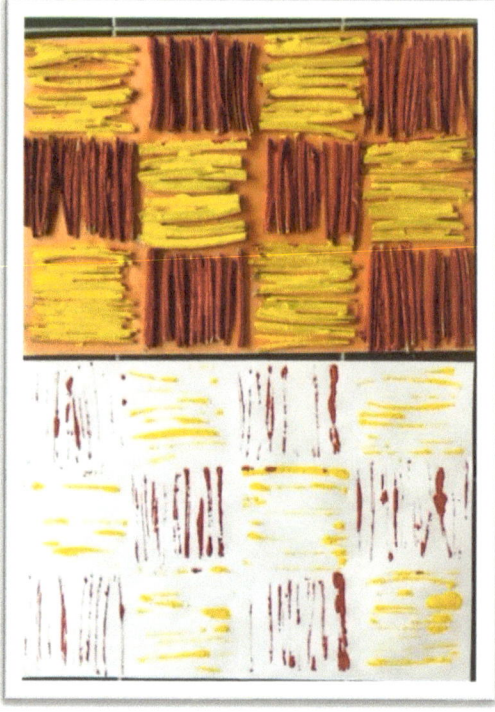

Patchwork twig pattern

Make a collection of straight twigs and cut them to roughly the same size.

Next, mark out a grid of squares on paper and help your child to glue them on to make a patchwork pattern as shown above.

Next you could paint the sticks in contrasting colours and make a print of the pattern – you could use this to make gift wrapping paper.

Twiggy the donkey

Make a cut-out donkey. I have used old grey tights to cover the body and legs to make a different texture. Use short bits of twig to make the mane – you could also add a twig tail.

Next, using your twigs from the garden, make a fence for the donkey paddock.

A log cabin in the trees

Make a log cabin using an old box. Cover the box with newspaper first as this will make it easier to glue your twigs on.

Next, using your twigs from the garden and small pieces of shrubbery, make miniature trees, pushing the pieces into a 'stand' made from plastercine or similer.

Twig picnic furniture

Make a table and chairs using twigs from the garden. The easiest way to do this is to use old boxes and cardboard tubes and glue the twigs on.

For the chairs, cut out two rectangular pieces from the bottom of a card tube leaving two curved stands as the legs. Next, cut down from the other end so that you have two long cuts roughly opposite each other that reach to just above the 'leg' height. Push one half into the other to make a seat. Now you can help your child cover the chair with glue and twigs (you could use straw or dried grasses).

For the table, use an old box and cut out four legs. Now you can stick on the twigs.

Add some miniature picnic food made from plasticine (or similar).

Bird's nest

Partly inflate a round balloon (about half way)

Next, put the balloon with the knot pointing down in a small box as a stand. Glue on strips of newspaper until about half of the balloon is covered – make two layers.

Next, using soft bendy twigs or strong grasses, bend and twist them to make loops that can be pushed down over the newspaper. Help your child to push short sticks into the gaps.

When the glue has dried, turn the balloon back upright and carefully pop and remove it.

If you have any moss in the garden, use it to line the inside of the nest.

Recycle play

Yoghurt pots

Yoghurt pots are a great alternative to commercial stacking cups. You can of course stack them and unstack them. You can build pyramids with them. You can paint them. You can put things in them and take things out. You can use them for sorting and for pouring in your water play.

Plastic milk cartons are a great resource. They can be painted and glued. You can fill them with interesting objects to create different sounds, and best of all they make great skittles – great for developing you child's throwing action.

Collect ten plastic drinks bottles with lids. Put a cupful of rice in each bottle to give it some stability (you could use water if you have no rice but screw the lids on tight!). Glue or tape labels on each bottle, with a number on each (1-10).

Set them up as skittles and take turns to knock them down with a soft ball. Ask your child to tell you which numbers they have hit.

Plastic bottles and tubs

Clear plastic bottles are another great resource. For some strange reason I have found children love playing with bottles like this, especially if they have bright coloured water in them. You just need to make sure the tops are on very tight!

As an alternative, you could fill them with different things, such as rice, salt, seeds, pasta, dried peas, or lentils and make them different weights. This is great for learning about 'heavy' and 'light' and of course they make great musical shakers for joining in when you're singing.

We seem to collect hundreds of these pots, used for dips and sauces. Because they are clear, unlike the yoghurt pots, they are better for sorting. What you use will depend on what you have in the house; if you have bricks and animals, you can sort those, otherwise you could use orange segments, raisins, or other safe pieces of fruit.

Boxes

There are lots of things you can do with boxes and used food packaging. You can make tunnels and bridges for toy cars, or homes with doors and windows for toy figures, beds, trains, rocket ships, boats, spaceships or just a tower that can be knocked down.

Here's the Hungry Monster box. Using a large box, make a hungry monster. Make a large opening for its mouth. Make large teeth, and give it eyes, nose, and ears.

The one in the picture eats numbers, but you could use it to eat anything. This can be used to help learn counting or sorting. If you remember to animate the Hungry Monster box, he will really come alive to your child, especially if you give him a voice.

I love egg boxes. Because of the small compartments you can put lots of different things in them and they open like a treasure box. They are great for a 'what's inside the egg box?' game.

It could be anything, but if you can set it up differently each time, you can generate real excitement and anticipation.

Here's another fun game. Fill a box with shredded paper and hide things in it. As your children get older you can put more things in and make them smaller and harder to find. Remember to close the box so that opening the box is part of the fun and anticipation.

If you have a selection of old bags or handbags, you can use them to hide objects in the same way. If you hide non-toy objects, such as an old bunch of keys, in the bags it can be more fun, especially if your children have no idea what you might have put inside.

Don't throw away those odd socks or buttons, make them into glove puppets.

Balancing

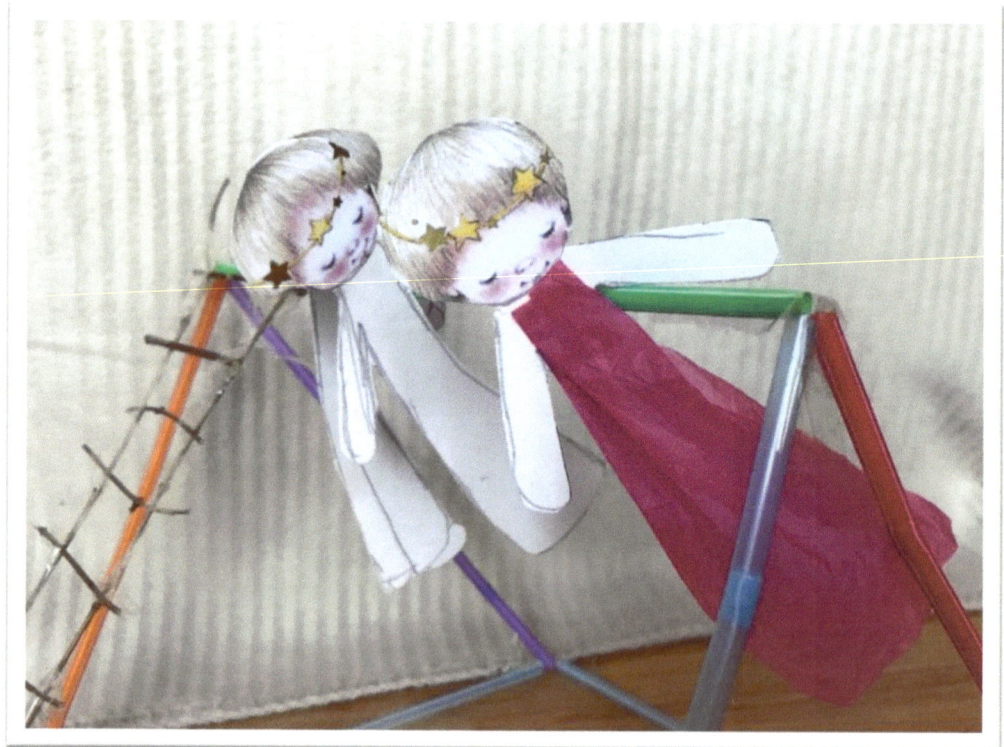

Balancing angels

Using card, such as the back of an old greeting card or cereal box, draw and cut out figures as shown below. They don't have to be exact copies but the portion of the cut out that is hanging down (the body in this case) must be longer than the top portion (the arm in this case).

Your child can draw a face or colour in the cut out (I have cut out some faces from old cards and stuck them on). If you have some coloured tissue paper, you could even dress them. You can then balance them on a pencil or finger or as in the picture on a straw. (I have made a triangular frame with straws and a twig ladder for them to climb up)

Rocking cat

Using folded card, such as an old greeting card (folded inside out) or cereal box (folded), draw and cut out the rocking cat shown above. I used a plate to draw around to get the smooth rocking edge.

Remember not to cut along the top edge or you will end up with two separate pieces! Draw, paint, or stick shapes to make the face. You could thread string, pipe cleaners or even old matchsticks to make the whiskers.

Balancing box

Ask your child to try to balance a small box on the edge of a table. Next, put a weight at one end inside the box (you could use a stack of coins or even a potato) and tape it in place. If you place the box on the edge of the table with the weighted end above the table, you will see it balance amazingly.

Decorating a magic balancing box

Find a small old box, carefully undo it so that you can turn it inside-out to make a blank box that can be decorated. Put a weight inside if you want it to be a balancing box before you decorate it. I used old greetings cards again and cut out small pictures and patterns and glued them on with a glue stick.

Balancing man

Using the inside of an old greeting card (or other piece of plain card folded), draw half a man against the folded edge so that when you cut round it you will have a symmetrical cut out. Your child can decorate and draw/stick on a face. Next you need two small coins of the same value (same weight) and stick them on the feet – I used a glue stick. Now your man will balance on your finger and even on a pencil or straw.

Balancing weights

Find a clothes hanger – preferably one with openings at each end where you can hook some string or cotton over. Next find two light plastic containers such as pots for dips or even yoghurt pots – make sure they are the same size. Next you need some string or cotton to attach the pots to the hanger. Ideally you need three or four evenly spaced places to

 attach your pots (if you only use two your pots may tip). Now your child can experiment to see which of their toys can balance.

Vehicles with wheels

Cart or car with wheels

Using old boxes and card, make seats for the inside of your vehicle and wheels. Depending on the size of your vehicle, you could use cocktail sticks, straws, or pencils as axels for your wheels. Remember to put something over the ends of the axels to stop the wheels falling off.

Bus with passengers

Using two pieces of card (the backs of greeting cards will do), put them on top of each other and draw a bus like the one shown above. Cut around the outline (both pieces at the same time so that you can have two opposite sides of a bus). Draw and cut out 4 or 5 windows – you could do this in both. Next cut as many strips of card as you want that you can feed through behind the windows. Using your cut-out windows as a template, draw windows on the strips.

Using a small box, glue or tape the top and bottom of each cut out so that your bus can stand up – be careful not to glue across where the windows are. Next you can either draw your passengers or cut them out from cards or magazines and stick them in the window shapes that you have drawn on the strips. Now you can choose which passengers are in the bus – just slide them in.

Train with shiny wheels

Cover some old card with a large piece of kitchen foil.

Help your child to draw and cut out the shape of a steam engine in black or dark paper. Cut out the window, funnel, fender and wheels and stick the silhouette onto the foil so that it shows through the holes. Cut a long thin piece for the rail.

Next the background can be painted.

Mixed materials train

Using some old paper and a washing up sponge, paint a background and let it dry.

Next, using plasticine (or similar) roll flat and cut out sections of a steam engine. Make a long thin sausage for the railway track.

Next find some old buttons for the wheels.

Train tracks game

Using either a large sheet of paper or smaller pieces taped together, help you child to paint it to look like grass or a meadow or fields where the train tracks will go.

Next make some 'stations'. For the stations, make large cut-out shapes that can be painted different colours. Make small copies to be the station 'tickets' that players collect when they land on the station.

When dry, glue these onto your background and help your child to paint a railroad track between the stations. Make the spaces between the sleepers large enough for a 'counter' to land on.

Next take turns to move your 'counters' according to the throw of the dice. The winner is the first person to collect all the shapes (or colours).

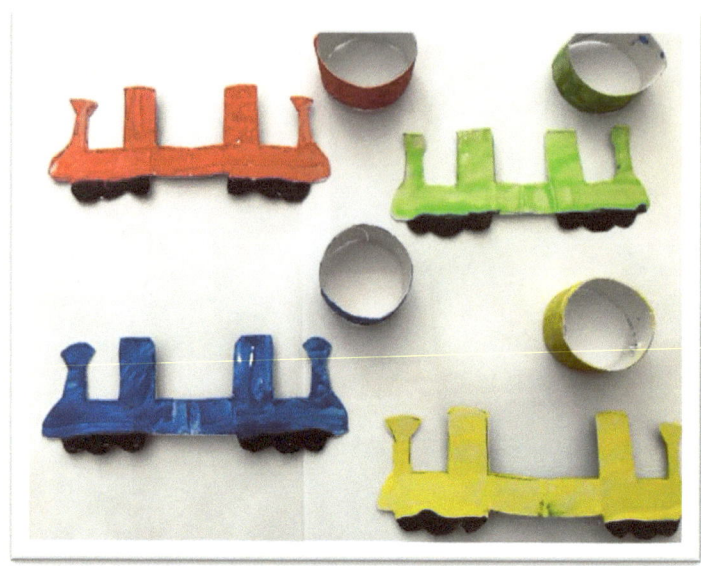

Miniature trains for your train track game

A carboard tube cut into quarters will give you four trains as 'counters' for your game.

Using some thin white card (I used an old food box) copy the train outline shown above – with the tab between the two images.

Fold it in half to cut it out so that both sides will look the same. Make four. Help your child to paint all the pieces.

When dry, the train shape can be glued to the card tube as shown and the miniature trains can go around the track for your game.

![An edible train made from cheese and crackers on a blue background](image)

An edible train

Make a train using different kinds of cheeses and crackers. (I have used Swiss cheese to make the holes for the clouds of steam.)

Mobiles and spinners

Spinning spiral

Find some spare card (I have used a cereal box). Using a plate, draw around it to get a circle. Cut out the circle. Next, working from the outside edge cut diagonally to about 2cm deep, then following the line of the edge of the circle, cut continuously at a width of 2cm in a spiral until you reach the centre. Attach cotton to the centre of the spiral. When you hold it up you should see it start to spin.

The spiral can be decorated with coloured shapes or stickers, or feathers etc. You could even make small lightweight cut outs to hang from it like a mobile.

Spinning colours

Using a paper plate, or circle of card, colour sections or patterns using felt pens or crayons. Find the centre of you circle. You can do this by drawing around you circle on scrap paper, cutting it out, and then folding it in half and then half again – the centre will be at the point where the two folds cross each other. Lay the paper over the card and poke a pencil through the paper and then into the card. Hold the pencil between two hands and spin it and watch the colours disappear.

The spinner can be decorated with coloured shapes stuck on as an alternative. The colours can be regular or placed at random as shown above – when spinning, the colours will still fade away.

Spinning windmill

For this you need a square of paper, a straight stick from the garden, two old buttons, and a paper clip. Fold the paper diagonally twice (so you have four triangle shapes). Next cut half-way along each of the folds. Next tape the four corners at the centre, overlapping each other. Next you need to thread a button at one end of the paper clip and push the extended wire through the centre of the paper (If you have some plasticine, or something similar, to push against, this will be safer and easier). Next thread the second button onto the wire before you attach it to your stick.

The windmill can be decorated before you assemble it.

Clown mobile

Find some old Christmas or birthday cards. If not, you could use newspapers or magazines but try to find colourful images and cut out two rectangles similar in shape to greetings cards. Fold one back and forth on itself – as if you were making a fan, but tie or tape it in the middle to make a bow tie. With the second card tape or tie two corners together to make a bishop-type hat.

Using a paper plate if you have one, make a happy face together. You could use broccoli stalks and grapes for the eyes and mouth, a carrot end for the nose or even part of an egg box. Next ask your child to change the face to make it sad.

If you have a printer, you could take photos of the face (one happy and one sad) cut them out and glue back-to-back and use it to make a mobile by attaching the hat to the top with cotton and the bow tie at the bottom with cotton. When the face spins you should see happy face – sad face etc.

Sun and clouds mobile

Using some stiff card or paper plates, help your child to paint both sides of two circles in two different yellows. Next cut out triangles around the edges of both circles. Stick the two large circles together, slightly off set so that the points of the triangles of one show through the gaps of the other, and then stick the triangles on, alternating the two colours as shown. Using more old card, cut out some cloud shapes and glue on a thin layer of cotton wool to make them fluffy. Now you can attach them to make a day-time mobile.

Sun and birds mobile

Using some stiff card or paper plates, make two suns, painting them yellow on one side and orange on the other then cutting out triangles as shown. The triangles can then be stuck on to the contrasting colour on both sides (half on each side). Make a cut toward the centre and a corresponding cut from the top to the centre in the second sun and slide one into the other as shown.

Next find some old card and cut out two bird shapes. Using coloured paper (the pink paper shown was from a Mother's Day envelope), cut out some leaf-shaped tail feathers, cutting fringes at the sides. Next cut out triangles in two contrasting colours and glue them on overlapping to give a feathered effect. Now they can be attached to the sun.

Moon mobile

Using some stiff card from a food box, cut out a large moon shape. Next, using a template such as a spice jar lid, draw circles in two or three different colours of thin paper. Help your child to cut them out.

These can then be glued on overlapping as shown in a sequence of two or more colours. Next, using thin card, cut out some stars. The stars in the picture have been covered with kitchen foil. Using cotton join your stars to the moon as shown.

Planet mobile

You will need some thick card (an old box will do). Cut out a circle and then an inner circle. Using some watery paint, and holding the centre of the inner circle with a cocktail stick, spin the circle while your child paints stripes of different colours.

Next (making sure you prepare for splashing) spin the card and watch the paint run towards the outer edge. Next your child can paint the 'Saturn' ring. Using cocktail sticks, attach the inner circle and outer ring by pushing the cocktail stick between the layers of card. You could attach some cotton to make a mobile.

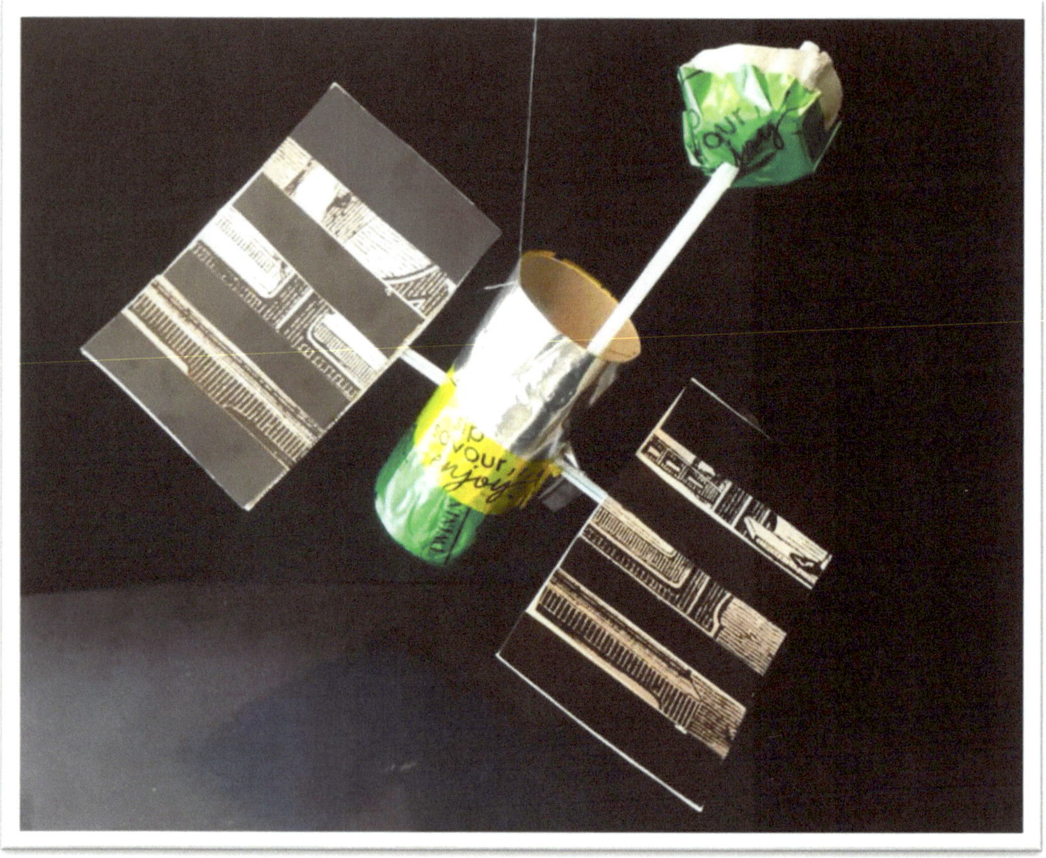

Satellite mobile

Cover a cardboard tube using a sequenc of coloured strips. I used the foil bags from a box of tea bags. The satellite transmitter dish is made from part of an egg box and a straw. To make the solar panels, cut strips of black and grey from magazines that can be stuck on alternately to two rectangular pieces of card (I used the box from the tea bags). These can then be attached to a straw that goes through the central tube. Attach with cotton to make a mobile.

Fishy mobile

Using old greeting cards, draw and cut out fish shapes, keeping the left over card from around your cut out. Cut out scale shapes from the left over card and stick them on to the blank side of your fish (starting from the tail end). Look for a good colour or shape to cut out your eyes (I used the wheel from a bus on the card).

Next, using a rectangle of some thin paper, fold it concertina style (like making a fan). Make a cut in your fish so that you can pass the folded paper through, then open it up to make fins. Join several fish with cotton to make a mobile. As an alternative, you could make scales out of sweet wrappers or kitchen foil.

Fish

Scales and fins

Using a large piece of old card, fold it in half and draw the outline of a fish. Cut it out, making sure that part of the top where the card is folded is left uncut. Next, using coloured paper, cut out scales. If you have two (or more) colours the scales can be stuck on in a sequence. Start at the tail end and overlap the scales. If you have enough scales, cover both sides. Next, using a cup-cake paper cup, cut it in half and stick one half on each side to make the fins.

Finally, if you have any old buttons these can be stuck on for the eyes. If your fish does not stand up by itself, use a paper clip to loosely attach the two halves at the bottom.

Mosaic whale message holder

For this use old cardboard, for example an old petfood box turned inside out. Next draw a whale on one side. Next cut out small squares of coloured paper; all the colours in the picture were from adverts in a magazine – you can find some really vibrant colours in magazines. Next stick them on with a glue stick.

Using pipe cleaners or bendy straws add a spout. Fold the card so that it makes an open triangular prism that will stand up and hold papers. You may need to tape it into place.

Fish shop

Using an empty drink carton, cut out three sides of a 'window', folding it inside to make a shelf. Ask your child to paint the outside. While the paint is drying, look through a magazine together to find a colourful advert. Cut out a rectangle and fold it concertina style to make the shop awning. Make a slit at the top of the carton and push your awning into it.

Next make some fish (or other food) to put in your shop. You could use plastercine or play dough, or paper cut outs etc.

Fishing game

Make some card fish cut outs (I used an old greeting card). Your child can decorate the fish and give them each an eye (one side will do). The more you can make the more fun the game will be. Next make a small hole where the fin would be. Using a small rubber band, tie a knot in one end and feed it through the hole so that you have a loop for a fin. Next, using straws and paper clips, open the paper clip at one end and close it at the other. Push the closed end up inside the straw. (To make the game more difficult, you could attach the paperclip hook with cotton or string.) Make a straw fishing hook for each player.

Next, using a cardboard tube (or one per player if you have enough resources), push paperclips through at random intervals to make hooks. Players pick up the fish by their fins and loop them onto the hooks on the pole. Make up your own rules according to the age of your child.

Rainbow fish

Draw the outline of a fish. Draw stripes across it. Next colour the stripes with something water based (I used felt pens, but paints are better). Next, using a clean paint brush and clear water, blend the colours together to give an under-water effect.

Noah's Ark

Using different kinds of bread, talk about their different textures – some bread is soft and spongy, some is hard and smooth, some is grainy etc.

Cut pieces of different kinds of bread into long strips so they look like long wooden planks and lay them together to make a Noah's Ark.

Space

Rocket made without glue

You will need three yoghurt pots, some old card, and a cardboard tube (from kitchen towel). First you need to make three wings using the card. A template is provided above. To give you an idea of scale, the bottom edge needs to be 4cm to fit into the top of a yoghurt pot. Help your child to paint the pots and card before you assemble your rocket.

When the paint is dry, cut out the three wings. Make a cut across the top of each of the yoghurt pots and push the base of each wing into the slit. Make sure it is a tight fit. Next make three slits in the cardboard tube and push in the wings (make sure this is a tight fit also). Finally, using a semicircle of paper or card, make a cone and push it into the top.

Spaceships on pegs

Using old cards and scraps of coloured paper, make spaceships small enough to fit onto wooden pegs.

Make a long 'fringe' of card and stick stars on to make the jet stream that follows the spaceships. When they are finished, stick them onto the pegs to peg onto a string or to decorate your book shelf.

Outer-space and astronaut

Using some thin card, cut a long fringe. Roll it up and bend the fringe pieces so that they splay outward. Next paint the underside and print onto dark coloured paper. Make one for each colour if you don't want the colours to mix.

Using old card, cut out an astronaut shape, separating the arms and legs (the boots can also be separated) so that you can put the astronaut in any position. Next wrap each part in foil. Cut out an opening in the helmet and put a piece of clingfilm across for the visor. You could use a face from an old card or better still a photo of your child or someone in the family. Position all your pieces on your background.

Rocket ship mosaic

Using an old food box, turn it inside out keeping the side flaps so that you can fold them back later to give your picture a box frame. Next draw a space rocket. Using old magazines, find coloured pieces to cut into squares to stick on as your mosaic. When finished, tape the flaps into place. Your picture can now be hung up on display.

The sky at night

Using an old food box, turn it inside out and fold it so that it makes a triangular prism with one side edge overlapping on the outside. Next tuck all the loose ends inside; this will keep the box from opening up again and shouldn't need any glue.

Find two (or more) contrasting colours to cut into long rectanlges so that your child can stick them on in sequence to make the bricks of the house. Next find two (or more) contrasting colours to cut into triangles so that your child san stick them on in sequence to make roof tiles.

Finally, make some moon, sun, and star shapes and stick them onto the ends of straws. Make holes in the roof and push the straws in.

Spring

A seasons tree

Either cut out or paint a tree silhouette with just a trunk, branches and twigs (no leaves).

Depending on which season you are in (it's Spring here) attach the appropriate items to your tree using a removable tac (blutac). For blossom, you could use scrunched up tissue paper.

Pocket gift card

Using an old pair of trousers or other item of clothing that has a pocket, cut out the pocket with enough surrounding material to stick it onto an old greeting card. Use more old cards to stick inside to cover where you have stuck down the edges of the fabric.

Next help your child to choose some old cards to cut into strips to make colourful book marks. Now you can choose what to stick on the top, for example your child could paint butterflies on one half folded over to make symetrical patterns as shown.

Spring flowers

Using old magazines, help your child to cut out circles of different colours or patterns (even photos of crowds of people that I have used can be effective). Glue them into position to make a flower. Next, open out a paper clip and thread on a button – the larger the better. Bend the wire back through the flower head so that you have both ends together. Push both ends of the wire through the centre of the flower head.

Using a straw (green if you have them) push the two ends of the paper clip wire down through the top of the straw. Next find some green (it only needs to be the narrow edge of an advert or picture) to make the leaves that can be taped onto the straw stems.

Mary, Mary, quite contrary,
how does your garden grow?
With silver bells, and cockle shells,
and pretty maids all in a row.

Contrary Mary's garden

Using old card, cut out large stalk and leaf shapes that can be painted and stuck on to paper.

Next, using some thinner card that is white on at least one side, cut out some flower heads. These can now be stuck on and painted – give them each a face.

Next, using the same card, cut out smaller stalks and leaves but only stick them down at the bottom so that you can hang the bells on. To make the silver bells, you just need a circle of kitchen foil (or a milk-bottle top) and mould it into shape around the end of your finger.

Next cut out and paint some shell shapes and fold them concertina-style. Now they can be stuck on at the bottom of your picture.

Pop-up-flower

Using an old yoghurt pot (or similar), make a small hole in the bottom (big enough for a straw to go through). Next cover and/or paint the pot. Using two straws, squash one straw and fold it in half (about half the length of the straw) and squeeze it inside the other straw to give you a long stick (or you could use a green garden stick if you have one).

Next cut out some leaves using thin paper (this can be painted) and tape them onto the straw so that they will flop open as the flower is pushed upwards. Next you need to make the flower head. I used some old card for the petals by cutting out a star shape and making a hole for the straw. I used part of an egg box for the inner section, making a hole for the straw. I then cut the end of the straw into thin strips for the stamen before painting it.

Now you can pull the flower deep into the pot and then pop it up and watch the leaves flop open.

Hairy caterpillar

Using old card, cut out large circles (use a cup to draw around).
I made 8 circles. Paint them alternate colours. Using thin paper cut out circles that are bigger than the card ones. (I used colourful pages from a magazine). Cut a fringe around the edge of the paper circles. Next trim off the bottom so that the circles have a flat edge.
Cut out two small circles of card for the eyes and paint on a mouth. Assemble your caterpillar as shown; now you can add some feet.

Take this opportunity to warn your child not to handle caterpillars directly as they can cause dangerous alergic reactions.

Foil-winged bugs

Using thin card such as an Easter egg box, cut out small pear shapes.

Keep the wrappers from your Easter eggs or sweets and carefully flatten them. Cut them into squares just big enough to cover the pear shapes that can be used as wings.

Make some plasticine (or similar) bugs with six legs and push the wings into the bodies.

Eggs and birds

Egg cups

Using an old egg box, cut out all six cup shapes.

Use half of them for the base and half for the cup.

Paint all the sections and then glue the cups to the bases.

Choose how to smooth the top edge of the cup, I have used plasticene, but you could use play dough, or self-hardening clay, or ribbon, or simply line with cup-cake paper. You could add further decorations by gluing on shapes or stickers, or simply painting dots in contrasting colours.

Hatching chicks

Save the empty egg shell (including the top) from you boiled eggs.

Cover or paint the bottom half of small yoghurt pots to put the empty egg shells in.

The chick bodies can be made out of cotton wool or paper towel. Put one drop of yellow food colouring into a small glass of water and let your child drop in either the cotton wool or piece of kitchen towel (about a quarter will do). Take the cotton wool or kitchen towel back out once they have absorbed the coloured water and squeeze out the excess. Pull or push them into two balls – a large one for the body and a small one for the head.

Next, cut out a diamond shape in yellow paper and fold in half for the beak and make two paper eyes.

Put your chick inside the empty shell and pop the lid on the top.

Stuffed hen

Cut out a hen shape from old card. Cut out separately a comb, and wattle, and a beak. Using old tights, push the body section inside and up to the toe.

Next, using cut pieces of the remaining tights, stuff the body and seal up at the tail end. Next, using old socks, cover the comb, wattle and beak and then glue them on. Add an eye.

Next make a stand using plasticine (or similar).

Vegetable printed chicks and hen

Using an old oval-shaped potato cut in half, help your child to print a hen body. Using the other half, cut out a shape for the comb and wattle for your child to print. A small carrot cut lengthways will make the legs and tail and beak.

Next, use either carrots or small parsnips cut in cross section to print the chicks and the sun.

Draw in the legs, beaks and eyes with a black felt pen. I have sprinkled some egg shell where the chicks have hatched.

Pop-up-bird

You will need a piece of rectangular card. Paint it orange. You will also need a piece of paper the same size.

Fold them both in half. With the piece of paper folded in half, cut at right angles in the middle of the fold a few centimeters. This can be folded to make the pop-up beak.

Next paint the beak and the body of the bird on the paper and let it dry.

Next cut out two paper heart shapes. Fold each one in half and cut a fring around the outer edge.

Using a straw, feed it through so that it goes past the back of the bird, then you can glue the wings onto the straw. Finally, stick the paper onto the orange card.

3D blackbird

Fold a piece of paper in half and draw half a bird shape with a tail, body, head and wing. Paint this in with black paint, then fold in half and press down to get a symmetrical picture of a bird.

Next cut a piece of thin card the same shape as the wings and with a narrow section connecting the two wings. Cut two slits in your picture so that the card wings can slot through as shown in the picture.

Next, using coloured strips of paper from a magazine, glue them on like feathers as shown in the picture. Add some eyes and a beak.

Seeds

Windmill seed picture

Using wild bird seed, or any other old seeds you may have, help your child to sort them into different colours or shades. Draw a windmill and decide which seeds will go in each section.

Glue them onto your picture.

Apple owls

Make thin slices through the centre of a large apple to make the owl heads. Using using further slices make the bodies, then using left-over pieces, cut out the feet and ears.

Before painting, take the pip eyes away and put them back when the paint is dry.

Paint a branch for the owls to perch on.

Sycamore seed helicopters

Help your child to paint a piece of paper with green and orange or brown using their fingers. Use thin paint so that the finger prints can be seen, so that it will look like veins on a leaf.

When the paint is dry, cut the paper into a rectangular piece about 15cm x 5cm.

Fold this lengthways in half, then open out again. Then fold it the other way (so that you have a folded cross).

Cut from one end to the middle, then fold the two pieces in opposite directions.

Next, leaving about 5mm below, make two small cuts, one each side so that you can fold the opposite end to make a stem. Tape a seed to this (as an alternative use a paper clip as a weight).

When you drop it, it should spin like a helicopter.

Vegetable printing

Using bell peppers, print some flowers. First cut out the top with the seeds and put to one side (keeping the seeds).

Next cut cross section of peppers of different sizes so that your child can print concentric shapes. Use the long edge to print the leaves.

Put a blob of paint in the middle of each flower and sprinkle in the seeds.

A seedy face

Using a large tomato, make thin cross-section slices for the eyes and use the round left-over piece for a nose.

Cut some edge pieces for a mouth.

Using a paper plate or circle of old card, put the tomato face on.

Next paint where the hair will go.

Using at least two different types of seeds from the garden, stick them alternatley onto the painted area to make the stripy hair. I have used seeds from a silver birch tree and a hebe shrub.

Finally add a blob of paint to the eyes.

Spots and stripes

Pasta man

Using dried fruit or pasta (on flour and water if you have no glue) make patterns or pictures. I have used three types of pasta and two types of dried fruit. Your child may find it easier if you draw a picture for them to follow.

Weaving a baby/dolls blanket

Using strips of two colours (cloth or paper), fix the ends of one colour onto a piece of card so that they lie next to each other. With the strips of the other colour, alternating where you start, weave between the fixed strips as shown in the picture.

Spots and stripes

Make a picture of a bee visiting a flower using only spots (circles) and stripes. Help your child to draw around and cut out large circles for the flower petals and the bee's wings. Next you will need smaller circles for the stamen (anther where the pollen is).

Help your child to cut stripes for the bee's body and wings.

Just stripes

Make a tiger with a background of stripes like the shadows cast by tall trees. Help your child to draw around and cut out a tiger shape (I copied from 'The Tiger who came to tea').

Next you will need to cut lots of stripes. If you don't have all the colours you want, paint sheets of paper with the desired colour first and allow time for them to dry (I had to do this for the brown).

Help your child to stick the stripes onto the tiger and then trim around the edges.

Just spots

Make a leopard with a background of spots with the shadows cast by tall trees. Help your child to draw around and cut out a leopard shape (I copied my tiger but made the head smaller and the tail drop down).

Next you will need to cut lots of circles. If you don't have all the colours you want, paint sheets of paper with the desired colour first and allow time for them to dry. Help your child to stick the spots onto the leopard.

Stripes and spots

Make a zebra with stripes, and a butterfly and a flower with spots. Help your child to draw around and cut out a zebra shape. Next you will need to cut lots of narrow strips for the stripes. If you don't have all the colours you want, paint sheets of paper with the desired colour first and allow time for them to dry. Help your child to stick the stripes onto the zebra and then trim around the edges.

Spots and stripes

Make a ladybird with spots, and a background of long grass. Help your child to draw around and cut out an insect body shape. Next cut out four large red circles and put them together as shown. Cut thin strips for the legs. Next you will need spots for the eyes and the wings.

Next you will need to cut lots of narrow strips for the stripes of grass. If you don't have all the colours you want, paint sheets of paper with the desired colour first and allow time for them to dry.

Imaginative play

Learning to eat is something your own child will already be familiar with. Children can role play being a parent feeding a baby at a very young age and even understand pretending to eat from a spoon themselves.

Have a pretend picnic, role play feeding the toys and each other and role play preparing the food, stirring something in a pan or in a bowl. You could even use real food such as pieces of fruit or crackers.

Here is another idea for using boxes. Create a maze or roadway that you can crawl along or through together. If you have pets, you might find they join in on this too – our cats love getting into these boxes!

Here the toys are in a train on their way to an adventure. It could also be a bus, a boat or even a space rocket.

Using your toys, tell a story using teddies or dolls as actors. For example, you could retell the three little pigs. You could even make costumes for them with your child's own clothes and even think about props and scenery – have fun with this yourself. If you animate the toys (make them move) your children will be captivated – you can even give them different voices.

Bear stories

Goldilocks and the three bears

Make your own teddy-bear puzzles in three different sizes with some old card and buttons. (Make the smallest one first and then draw around it to get the next size up; cut out the muzzle as separate pieces for your child to match up the correct sizes)

The Teddy Bears' Picnic

Using old greeting cards, try to find pictures of teddy bears (or other animals that can be invited to the picnic) and cut them out. Using plasticine or blue-tac, make stands so that your cut outs can stand up.

You could use some cloth or a book for a background (or even take them outside if the weather is suitable) and set them up together to look as if they are having a picnic.

Miniature outside for the teddy bears' picnic

Find an old box. Turn it on its side and make a hole in what is now the top (about the size of a finger). Find some things from outside. If you cut the ends off shrubs, they can be made to look like trees. Stones can be used as seats or tables. If you still have your cut-outs and plasticine stands, they can be placed inside. By shining a torch through the hole (a mobile/cell phone light works well) you can make it look as if the sun is shining on your scene.

The three bears

Using coloured paper or card (old greetings cards will do), make a pile of triangles of different sizes. Arrange them so that they are bears of different sizes.

Jack and the beanstalk

Jack's beanstalk

Using some old sheets of paper, cut them into strips about 10cm deep (half a sheet of A4). Tape the strips together to make a long piece – the longer the strip the taller the beanstalk. Paint it shades of green and leave to dry. Next you need to cut out some leaf shapes about 8cm long. You could use green paper, but they would look better painted if you have time for them to dry.

When dry, tape or glue your leaves to the top edge of the long strip about 4 cm onto the strip (so that they poke over the edge). Next, you need to tightly roll the whole thing up with the leaves on the outside of the roll. Tape the end down.

Next help your child to carefully pull up the roll from the inside and watch your beanstalk grow. (Be carefull not to over extend or it will unwind itself).

Jack and the Beanstalk game

Using some old sheets of paper, put them together to make one long piece. Using an old washing-up sponge, help your child to cover the paper with blue paint to create a cloudy sky.

Next paint a long and winding beanstalk. Cut out leaves and write the numerals on 1-10. If you have enough leaves (20) do this twice.

Now you are ready to play the game. Using counters for each player, roll dice and move up the stalk the number of leaves that you have rolled. Read the number that you have landed on and then, like Jack, go and collect things from the giant's castle – the same number of things as shown on the leaf. (You could put your own treasure in boxes before the game)

The winner could be the first person to the top of the stalk, or if your child is good at counting, the person who has collected the most objects.

The harp from the giant's castle

Using some old card that can be folded (I used a delivery packet), draw the shape of a harp. Draw in some jewels for your child to colour in with thick crayon. Next the harp can be painted with watery yellow paint so that the jewels stand out.

When your harp is dry, cut it out (without cutting the bottom edge – it can be a base). Using either straws or cocktail sticks attach thread or elastic bands - if you have long and loose ones.

The goose that laid the golden eggs

Paint a background using thick green paint for the grass. To make the blades of grass effect, use a fork to scrape through the paint.

On a separate piece of paper, draw a goose – like a duck but with a longer neck. To get the brown feathery effect, use an old washing up sponge – practise getting the right amount of paint on a spare sheet or old newspaper. Don't worry if you go over the edges.

Cut out your goose and place her in the grass. You could add some golden eggs.

The giant's treasure chest

Try to find an old box with a lid so that you can actually open it. Help your child to paint the box brown to make it look like wood.

Next, using some old card, cut it to the same length as your box, but bend it round (with flat flaps underneath) so that it makes a curved lid. Paint it brown to match the box. To stop your lid unravelling, use an elastic band at each end.

To make the padlock, attach a paper clip to another elastic band. Wrap the paper clip in kitchen foil and poke a hole through for the key hole. Glue the curved lid to the top of the box.

Finally cut circles of foil and wrap them tightly around the bottom corners of the box (you might need to glue them into place).

The story of The Great Big Enormous Turnip

The great big enormous turnip

Using some old card made into a long strip (about half a metre), paint it brown to make the earth. Make a wobbly cut to push your turnip into later.

Next cut out a large card turnip shape. Cut out a small hole (like a cup handle) at the side. Next cut out a paper turnip using the card as a template so that it covers your card turnip. Glue it to the card (except across the handle) and paint it purple.

Next make some long floppy leaves and glue them to the top of the turnip.

When it's dry, push the bottom pointed end of the turnip into the wobbly slot.

You will need to keep this so that you can add to it.

The old man pulled and the old woman pulled...

Using some old card cut out the shape of an old man with outstretched arms and an old woman.

Next find some old frabric or paper and cut out items of clothing and glue them on (the toe end of an old sock makes a great hat).

You can hook the old man's hands onto the edge of the turnip where you left the handle. If you make a similar 'handle' on the man you can hook the old woman's hands onto him.

You will need to keep this so that you can add to it.

... and the little girl pulled, and the dog pulled...

Using some old card cut out the shape of a little girl with outstretched arms and a dog.

Next find some old frabric or paper and cut out items of clothing and glue them on to the little girl. If you have some old fur fabric that would be great for the dog – I have used some old scraps of wool.

You will need to keep this so that you can add to it.

The dog called the ginger cat, and they pulled...

Using some thin old white card, cut out the shape of a cat.

If you have some old fur fabric that would be great for the cat – I have used some old scraps of wool.

You will need to keep this so that you can add to it.

The cat called the mouse and they pulled and pulled, and up came the giant turnip at last!

Using some thin old white card, cut out the shape of a mouse.

Because the mouse is quite small I found it easiest to paint it.

Next you need a long piece of string. Tie it to the 'handle' that you cut out on the turnip then attach all the characters to the string – you could glue or tape them or thread the string through.

Finally, help your child to pull the string and watch the turnip come up out of the ground.

Old MacDonald's Farm

Old MacDonald's Farmhouse

Using an old box, either paint it or turn it inside out to get an even brown colour.

Using pages from a magazine or any other scraps of coloured paper, cut out small blue squares for the windows and small white strips for the window frame. Help your child to glue them into place.

Using another old piece of card, cut a piece big enough to make the roof. To make the roof tiles, cut circles and glue them on overlapping, starting with the bottom edge. To make the top edge, cut the circles in half.

Next make a fence using more old card – this can be painted.

(Keep this if you can)

Old MacDonald had some cows...

Use a card tube and some old flat card. Cut a long strip of card just wide enough to fit through the card tube. Push it through and bend the ends down making sure they are the same length. Next cut out a triangle at each end to make the cows legs. Next cut out a head shape with two long tabs each side as shown in the picture. Take the legs back out for your child to paint along with the face and body. When dry, the legs can be pushed back in and the tabs for the head pushed in at one end.

Now you can put her in the farmyard.

Old MacDonald had some pigs...

Use a card tube and some old flat card. Cut the tube in half so that you have two short tubes. Cut a strip of card just wide enough to fit through each card tube. Push it through and bend the ends down making sure they are the same length. Next cut out a triangle at each end to make the legs (these need to be shorter than the cow's).

Next cut out a head shape with two long tabs each side as shown in the picture. Take the legs back out for your child to paint along with the face and body. When dry, the legs can be pushed back in and the tabs for the head pushed in at one end.

Now you can put them in the farmyard.

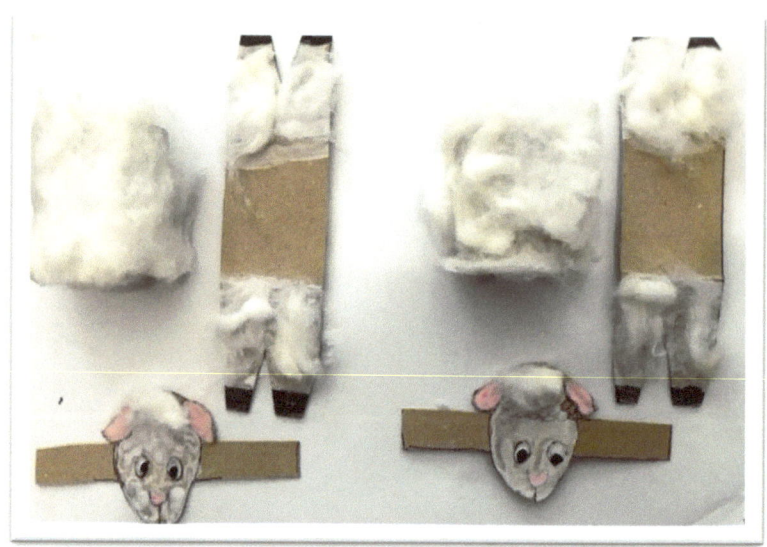

Old MacDonald had some sheep...

Use a card tube and some old flat card. Cut the tube in half so that you have two short tubes. Cut a strip of card just wide enough to fit through each card tube. Push it through and bend the ends down making sure they are the same length. Next cut out a triangle at each end to make the legs (these need to be shorter than the cow's).

Next cut out a head shape with two long tabs each side as shown in the picture. Take the legs back out for your child to paint along with the face and body. You could add some cotton wool – it will stick to the wet paint. When dry, the legs can be pushed back in and the tabs for the head pushed in at one end.

Now you can put them in the farmyard.

Old MacDonald had some ducks...

Use a card tube and some old flat card. Cut the tube into short pieces so that you can have several ducks. Cut out feet with a central tab as shown, and a diamond for the beak.

Next cut out a head shape with two long tabs each side as shown in the picture. Help your child to paint all the pieces.

To put it together, fold the feet in and tuck them underneath. Make a small slit where the mouth would be, fold the diamond in half and push it through the slit from the back point first to make the beak. Make a small vertical slit at the front of the section of tube and push through the flaps for the head.

Lightning Source UK Ltd.
Milton Keynes UK
UKHW050013070722
405433UK00005B/93